# NOTES

ON THE

# TURKISH ARMY,

WITH A SHORT

# VOCABULARY

OF TURKISH WORDS AND PHRASES

1915

The Naval & Military Press Ltd

*Published by the*
# The Naval & Military Press

Unit 10 Ridgewood Industrial Park,
Uckfield, East Sussex, TN22 5QE
Tel: +44 (0) 1825 749494
Fax: +44 (0) 1825 765701

MILITARY HISTORY AT YOUR FINGERTIPS
www.naval-military-press.com

ONLINE GENEALOGY RESEARCH
www.military-genealogy.com

ONLINE MILITARY CARTOGRAPHY
www.militarymaproom.com

*In reprinting in facsimile from the original, any imperfections are inevitably reproduced and the quality may fall short of modern type and cartographic standards.*

# TABLE OF CONTENTS.

| | PAGE |
|---|---|
| *Notes on the Turkish Army—* | |
| Organization | 3 |
| Cavalry | 4 |
| Artillery | 4 |
| Infantry | 5 |
| Uniform | 6 |
| Machine guns | 6 |
| Transport, &c. | 6 |
| Engineers | 7 |
| Reserve army | 7 |
| "Ordre de Bataille" | 9 |
| Military titles | 12 |
| Badges of rank | 13 |
| Rations and forage | 14 |
| Decorations | 15 |
| | |
| *Civil Administration* | 1 |
| Gendarmerie | 16 |
| Religious persons | 16 |
| Police (civil and military) | 17 |
| Notes for troops in regard to the civil population | 18 |

## APPENDICES.

| | PAGE |
|---|---|
| Appendix I.—Glossary of military terms | 22 |
| " II.- Turkish coinage, weights and measures | 25 |
| Distance and time | 27 |
| III.—Turkish vocabulary and phrases | 28 |

# NOTES ON THE TURKISH ARMY.

*Organization.*—The Turkish army, which suffered to a very great extent both in men and material during the last Balkan wars, has since then been reorganized, and the army itself, both officers and men, have undergone a severe course of training under the supervision of German officers headed by General Liman von Sanders.

Although a great improvement has taken place during the last two years, it cannot truthfully be said that Turkish troops are even now in any way equal, except in courage, to those of the Balkan States with whom they were lately at war.

Prior to 1910 the Christians in the Ottoman Empire were exempt from service, but since that year all Ottoman male subjects are liable for military service, irrespective of their religion, for a period of 25 years from 1st March following their 20th birthday. A certain number of these are still exempt from service, *e.g.*, judges and students of Moslem law and theology, non-Moslem priests, &c., and Moslem immigrants of less than 6 years' residence in the Empire. The system of buying exemption by paying a tax of £T40 to £T60 in lieu of service, which obtained for the Christian population prior to 1910, was supposed to have disappeared when the law alluded to above was passed, but it evidently still exists, for there is evidence to show that a large sum of money was paid to the Imperial exchequer in this respect during the mobilization of 1914.

By the Military Law of 1914 the duration of service in the Turkish Army is roughly as follows :—

(1.) Active Army (*Nizam*) ... ... 2 years.
    (3 years for cavalry and artillery.)
(2.) Active Army Reserve (*Redif*) ... 16 „
(3.) Territorial Army (*Mustafiz*)... ... 7 „

The Active Army consists of 13 army-corps and 2 independent divisions (Asir and Hejaz). Each of these corps, with the exception of the 7th, 12th and 13th, are composed of 3 divisions, the exceptions being 2 division corps. There are 3 regiments in each division (except the Asir independent division, which has only 2 regiments), and each regiment on mobilization consists of 3 battalions. Consequently, the Active Army on mobilization consists of 38 divisions, 113 regiments, and 339 battalions. In addition to the above number of battalions, 113 depôt battalions (one battalion per regiment) are formed on mobilization. These depôt battalions are subdivided into a number of companies corresponding with the number of battalions composing the regiment, *i.e.*, 3 companies per depôt battalion.

There used to be a certain number of "Nishanji" (rifle) battalions, but these have now disappeared. On the other hand, 13 "Model" N.C.O. battalions, one per corps, have been created.

*Cavalry.*—The mobilized cavalry strength of the active army consists of 23 regiments, each regiment consisting of 5 squadrons (with the exception of that allotted to the 7th Corps, which has only 3 squadrons). To the 1st, 2nd, 3rd, 9th and 11th Corps are allotted one three-regiment brigade each, the remaining corps having only one regiment each.

In addition to the regular cavalry, there are several irregular regiments of Kurdish cavalry with an estimated strength of about 20,000, but nothing is known with regard to their formation or equipment

The cavalry are armed with the 7·65-mm. Mauser carbine, and the 1st Lancer Regiment carry lances in addition.

*Artillery.*—The artillery is composed of 38 regiments, with numbers corresponding to the 38 divisions to which they are allotted. Each artillery regiment was supposed to consist of 3 three-battery groups, but owing to lack of material these were reduced to 3 two-battery groups, *i.e.*, 2 two-battery groups of field artillery and 1 two-battery group of mountain artillery. The actual allotment of artillery units to the Army Corps varies to some extent, but that shown in the "Ordre de Bataille" is the allotment which existed in October, 1914.

There is no heavy artillery with the field army.

There are only 24 horse artillery guns, which are allotted in two-battery groups, one each to the 1st, 9th and 11th

Corps. There are 17 four-gun field howitzer batteries, the allotment of which is shown in the "Ordre de Bataille."

The majority of the field artillery guns are old pattern 7·5-cm. Schneider, Creusot and Krupp guns, but the Germans have lately supplied a certain quantity of modern quick-firers. It is, therefore, impossible to estimate the number of guns with the Turkish army at the present time, but 1,000 field and mountain guns and 70 field howitzers can be considered a very liberal estimate. The field howitzer guns are—10·5-cm. Q.F. and 12-cm., old pattern. In addition there are also some 15-cm. howitzers, old pattern, which were obtained from Krupp during the last Balkan war. (N.B.—Quick-firer batteries are composed of 4 guns, old pattern of 6 guns per battery.)

The fortress artillery is not dealt with in these notes.

*Infantry.* — The war establishment of a battalion is (exclusive of transport) 1,081 officers and men, but the *effective* strength in the last operations before the present war was only about 24 officers and from 600 to 800 men. In the "Ordre de Bataille" it has been taken at the round figure of 1,000 of all ranks.

The battalion is composed of 4 companies; each company consisting of 4 officers and 261 men.

In addition, each battalion has a staff composed of :—

1 Major.
1 Aide de Camp (Lieutenant).
1 Medical Officer.
1 Surgeon.
1 Apothecary.
1 Chaplain (*Imam*).
1 Secretary (*Tabur kiatibi*).
1 armourer.
1 assistant secretary (serjeant-major).
1 serjeant clerk.
1 battalion storekeeper (serjeant-major).
1 assistant to above (corporal).
1 serjeant bugler.
2 corporal buglers.
5 officers' servants.

On mobilization 25 transport drivers and a serjeant to command the 2nd line transport are added.

The staff of a regiment (3 battalions) is:—

1 Colonel or Lieutenant-Colonel.
1 Aide-de-Camp (Lieutenant).
1 Secretary (*Alai kiatibi*), who is also Secretary for the 1st battalion.
1 Chaplain (*Alai Imami*), who is also Chaplain for the 1st battalion.
1 colour bearer (serjeant).
1 serjeant clerk.
1 assistant clerk (private).
1 orderly serjeant.
4 officers' servants.
1 transport driver (on mobilization).

13
—

The infantry are armed with 7·65-mm. Mauser rifle (1903 pattern) and short bayonet. Each man carries 120 rounds of small-arm ammunition on him.

*Uniform.*—The field service uniform is khaki with collar patches of various colours denoting the branch of the service. On the right-hand side of the collar patch is borne the number of the regiment, and on the left-hand side is the number of the company to which the man belongs.

*Machine guns.*—Machine gun companies (4 guns per company) are allotted to certain but not all regiments (*see* "Ordre de Bataille," page 9.)

*Other Organizations.*—In general, each army corps has the following additional organizations:—

1 transport battalion of 4 companies.
1 train battalion of 4 companies.
  N.B.—The 7th, 12th and 13th Corps have only 3-company battalions of the above.
1 telegraph company.
1 aviation detachment (1st, 4th, 9th and 10th Corps only).
1 technical section.
1 N.C.O. model battalion.
  N.B.—The two independent (21st and 22nd) Divisions of Asir and Hejaz have one telegraph and one train company only.

*Engineers.*—Under the new scheme of re-organization there should be one pontoon section to each division, one field battalion and telegraph company to each army corps, and an independent company to each independent battalion.

In addition to the above there are attached to the fortress of Adrianople an engineer battalion of 4 companies, a pontoon train of 3 sections, and a telegraph company. There is also a submarine mining battalion attached to the Dardanelles and Bosphorus defences. This latter force now includes a large number of German N.C.Os. and men.

*Reserves.*—The reserve formations can be divided into three classes, viz. :—

(1.) Reserve of active army (*Ihtiyat*).
(2.) Reserve army (*Redif* 1st and 2nd class)
(3.) Territorial army (*Mustahfiz*).

No. 1 consists of men who have served 3 years in the *Nizam* army, and corresponds more or less to the Reserve of the British Army. On mobilization they are used to complete the cadres of the active army and to form the depôt battalions already mentioned.

Of No. 2 the 1st class *Redif* is composed of men who have served 9 years with the colours (*Nizam* and *Ihtiyat*). They do not correspond to the second line troops of other armies, for they consist largely of matured men between the ages of 29 and 38 years, and are consequently of equal if not of superior value to the *Nizam*. On mobilization they are formed into 38 divisions corresponding to the active army, and these divisions are numbered accordingly. The uniform is the same as that of the *Nizam* army, but is distinguished by a black line at the bottom of the collar. The 2nd class *Redif* differ materially from the 1st Class, for they have not served in the regular army and have had very little military training. There are 19 divisions of this *Redif*, the distribution in regiments and battalions corresponding to that of the 1st class. The uniform is by way of being the same.

Up to date of going to press it is believed that seven reserve corps have been formed, namely, the 1st, 2nd, 3rd, 4th, 5th, 6th, and 8th, of which the first five are operating in Western Asia Minor and European Turkey, and the two last-named in Eastern Asia Minor.

No. 3 is a "levée en masse" of all trained men, and corresponds to the "Landsturm" of continental armies. They are used for filling up gaps in the *Redif* formations and for local garrison work.

*Ordre de Bataille.*—The "Ordre de Bataille," which is shown in tabulated form, takes no notice of depôt battalions or of any reserve formations. It is drawn up to exhibit the full mobilized strength of the *Nizam* field army, and includes *all* the field artillery armaments which, as far as is known, are available for the *whole* Turkish army. In order, therefore, to arrive at the total resources in fighting men which the Turks can possibly put in the field, another 600,000 should be added for 1st and 2nd class *Redifs*. The strength of the *Mustahfiz* or Territorial army is impossible to calculate with any degree of accuracy, for it is not organized in peace and many of the men thereof are taken to fill up the *Redif* formations in time of war. The grand total, however, of about 1,250,000 can be taken as a liberal estimate of the full strength of the whole Turkish army.

*March*, 1915.

# "ORDRE DE BATAILLE."

## MOBILIZED STRENGTH OF TURKISH ARMY.

Abbreviations—
F.A. = Field Artillery.  M.A. = Mountain Artillery.  F.H. = Field Howitzer.
H.A. = Horse Artillery.  Q.F. = Quick-Firer.  O.P. = Old Pattern.

| Army corps. | Peace Headquarters | Divisions | Titular numbers of regiments. | Number of battalions. | Infantry. | F.A. and M.A. guns. | F.H. guns. | Cavalry. | H.A. guns. | Machine guns. | Total strength. |
|---|---|---|---|---|---|---|---|---|---|---|---|
| I. | Constantinople | 1, 2, 3 | 70, 71, 124; 1, 5, 6; 7, 8, 9 | 27 | 27,000 | 72 Q.F. | 12 | 1,500 | 8 | 24 | 40,000 |
| II. | Adrianople | 4, 5, 6 | 10–12; 13–15; 16–18 | 27 | 27,000 | 72 Q.F. | 12 | 1,500 | … | 24 | 40,000 |
| III. | Gallipoli | 7, 8, 9 | 19–21; 22–24; 25–27 | 27 | 27,000 | 72 Q.F.* | 8 | 1,500 | … | 24 | 40,000 |
| IV. | Smyrna | 10, 11, 12 | 28–30; 126, 127, 33; 31–36 | 27 | 27,000 | 64 Q.F. | 12 | 500 | … | 20† | 40,000 |

\* 1 battery not yet formed.
† 1 company not yet equipped

"Ordre de Bataille"—continued.

| Army corps. | Peace Headquarters. | Divisions. | Titular numbers of regiments. | Number of battalions. | Infantry. | F.A. and M.A. guns. | F.H. guns. | Cavalry. | H.A. guns. | Machine guns. | Total strength. |
|---|---|---|---|---|---|---|---|---|---|---|---|
| V. | Angora | 13, 14, 15, 16 | 4, 37, 38; 40–42; 43–45; 125, 47, 48 | 27 | 27,000 | 64 Q.F. | 12 | 500 | ... | 24 | 40,000 |
| VI. | Aleppo | 24, 26, 39, 40 | 2, 3, 72; 76–78; 115–117; 118–120 | 27 | 27,000 | 56 Q.F. / 18 O.P. | ... | 500 | ... | 24* | 40,000 |
| VII. | Yemen (San'aa) | 23, 25 | 67–69; 73–75 | 18 | 18,000 | 48 O.P. | 12† | 300‡ | ... | 16 | 22,000 |
| VIII. | Damascus | 27, 17 | 79–81; 49–51 | 27 | 27,000 | 24 Q.F. / 48 O.P. | ... | 500 | ... | 24* | 40,000 |
| IX. | Erzerum | 28, 29 | 82–84; 85–87 | 27 | 27,000 | 72 O.P. | ... | 1,500 | 8 | 24 | 40,000 |
| X. | Sivas | 30, 31, 32 | 88–90; 91–93; 94–96 | 27 | 27,000 | 60 O.P. | ... | 500 | ... | 24§ | 40,000 |
| XI. | Kharput | 18, 33, 34 | 53, 98, 102; 52, 97, 99; 54, 100, 101 | 27 | 27,000 | 60 O.P. | ... | 1,500 | 8 | 24‖ | 40,000 |

| | | | | | | | | | |
|---|---|---|---|---|---|---|---|---|---|
| XII. | Mosul | ... | {35, 36 | 103-105, 106-108 | }18 | 16,000 | 72 O.P. | ... | 500 | ... | 16¶ | 25,000 |
| XIII. | Bagdad | ... | {37, 38 | 109-111, 112-114 | }18 | 18,000 | 54 O.P. | ... | 500 | ... | 16 | 25,000 |
| Ind. Div. | Asir | ... | 21 | 121, 122 | 6 | 6,000 | 24 O.P.** | ... | ... | ... | 8 | 7,000 |
| Ind. Div. | Hejaz | ... | 22 | 128-130 | 9 | 9,000 | 24 O.P. | ... | ... | ... | 12 | 10,000 |
| | Total | ... | 88 | ... | 339 | 339,000 | 904 | 68 | 11,300 | 24 | 304 | 489,000 |

\* 4 companies not yet equipped.
† Includes 1 mountain howitzer and 1 mountain battery
‡ 3 squadrons only.
§ 1 company not yet equipped.
‖ 2 companies not yet equipped.
¶ No companies yet equipped.
\*\* 1 battery not yet formed.

N.B.—All figures in the Turkish army must be regarded as approximate only.
NOTES.—In addition there are 108 depôt battalions, i.e., 1 battalion per regiment.
Q.F. batteries consist of 4 guns each.
O.P. batteries consist of 6 guns each.

## Military Titles.

The following are the principal titles and grades with their equivalents in the British service:—

### Officers.

| | |
|---|---|
| Mushir | Field-Marshal. |
| Birinji ferik | General. |
| Ferik | Lieutenant-general. |
| Liva | Major-general. |
| Miralai | Colonel. |
| Kaimakam | Lieutenant-colonel. |
| Bimbashi | Major. |
| Yuzbashi | Captain. |
| Mulazim-i-evvel | Lieutenant. |
| Mulazim-i-sani | Second-lieutenant. |
| Alai emini (or) Tabur emini. | Paymaster (regimental or battalion). |
| Sanjakdar | Standard bearer. |
| Bairakdar | Colour bearer. |
| Alai kiatibi (or) Tabur kiatibi. | Secretary (regimental or battalion). |
| Esswāb emini | Quartermaster. |
| Erkan-i-harb zabiti | Staff officer. |
| Yaver | Aide-de-camp. |
| Tabib | Medical officer called *Firka tabibi, Liva tabibi, Alai tabibi*, according to rank. |
| Jerrah | Surgeon. |
| Baitar | Veterinary surgeon. |
| Mufti (or) Imam | Moslem chaplain (regimental or battalion). |
| Evzaji | Apothecary. |

NOTE.—*A rank of "Kol aghassi," mid-way between Bimbashi and Yuzbashi, existed until recently, and officers bearing this title are still met with.*

### Non-commissioned Officers and Men.

| | | |
|---|---|---|
| Bash chaoush | | Serjeant-major. |
| ,, ,, | mu'avini | Assistant Serjeant-major. |
| Chaoush | | Serjeant. |
| Onbashi | | Corporal. |

| | |
|---|---|
| Buluk emini ... | ... Quartermaster - serjeant (now abolished and being replaced by Bash chaoush mu'avini). |
| Na'alband ... | ... Farrier. |
| Tufekji ... | ... Armourer. |
| Boruzan ... | ... Bugler. |
| Nefer ... ... | ... Private. |
| Piada neferi ... | ... ,, (infantry). |
| Suwari neferi | ... Trooper. |
| Topji neferi ... | ... Gunner. |
| Istihkiam neferi | ... Sapper. |
| Kazmaji ... | ... Pioneer. |
| Laghimji ... | ... Miner. |
| Timarji ... | ... Hospital assistant. |

BADGES OF RANK.

(*See* Plates at end of Book.)

The rank of officers is shown in general by the shoulder cords, though there are also some other minor distinctive marks in full dress. The shoulder cords are of universal pattern, and are worn equally with the service jacket, the tunic and the great-coat; they are gilt for combatant branches, silver for non-combatants. The design of the lace is of three different kinds, one for generals, one for field officers and the third for officers below that rank. White stars differentiate the grades within these three groups of ranks. Thus:—

| | | | |
|---|---|---|---|
| 3 stars denote marshal | — | | *kol aghassi* |
| 2 ,, ,, general | colonel | | captain |
| 1 star denotes lieutenant-general | lieutenant-colonel | | lieutenant |
| No ,, ,, major-general | major | | 2nd lieutenant |

The minor distinctive marks, also worn in full dress, are increased gold braiding on the cuffs and collar of the tunic for general and field officers: thick gold fringe on the general's epaulettes, thin fringe on those of field officers and plain epaulettes for officers below that rank.[*]

Capes are sometimes worn by officers, in which case the stars denoting rank are shown on collar patches of the distinctive colour.

---

[*] Epaulettes are worn in full dress on special occasions, instead of the shoulder strap.

*Non-commissioned officers* are distinguished from rank and file by having coloured shoulder straps, of distinctive colour for the arm to which they belong. To distinguish the various grades of non-commissioned officers, broad transverse bands are added (gilt for combatant ranks, silver for non-combatant). Serjeants have one band, assistant serjeant-majors two bands and serjeant-majors three bands. Corporals have no band.

The shoulder straps are bordered with red edging, and serjeant-majors also wear a red tassel to their side-arms.

A further distinction of bands of distinctive colour above the cuffs is also now being introduced; in this case a corporal will have one broad band, a serjeant one broad and one narrow, an assistant serjeant-major two broad, and a serjeant-major three broad bands.

## RATIONS AND FORAGE.

As a rule the soldier is fairly well fed. The ration comprises:—

Bread, 300 dirhems ($2\frac{1}{4}$ lb.).
Mutton, 100 dirhems ($\frac{3}{4}$ lb.).
Rice (about) 30 dirhems ($\frac{1}{4}$ lb.).
Onions, small quantities.
Salt.
Raisins, dried fruits.
Vegetables (lentils, beans, peas, potatoes, &c.).
Cooking butter.

Meat is given five days a week, and a pilaf of rice and dried fruits on the other days.

The bread is issued in flat loaves of one ration each.

Two meals per diem are provided, one in the forenoon and one in the afternoon; generally a meat stew is made, cooked in a large copper cauldron 2 feet in diameter and 1 foot deep, tinned inside and provided with a cover. Each man is provided with a copper dish 18 inches in diameter and 3 to 4 inches deep, and eats with a wooden spoon.

The cost of this ration is about 17*s.* a month, which is the unit of ration allowance for junior officers. The unit for senior officers consists of the first four articles, and costs 12*s.* a month.

*Forage.*—The usual ration is 9 lbs. of barley (*arpa*), given in two feeds, and 11 lbs. of chopped straw (*saman*), or hay in European Turkey.

DECORATIONS.

The principal decorations are the Mejidieh, Osmanieh, and Imtiaz.

*Mejidieh.*—Five classes. The badge is a seven-pointed silver order with red enamel in centre; ribbon red, green edges.

*Osmanieh.*—Four classes. The badge is a seven-pointed order in green enamel, red centre with crescent; ribbon green, red edges.

*Imtiaz.*—The Imtiaz has three classes. It is an order consisting of two medals, which can be conferred either separately or together; large gold and silver medal; ribbon red and green in two parallel bands. The star of the 1st class is eight-pointed.

*Iftikhar and Liakat.*—These distinctions nominally granted for merit and valour, have been distributed rather as bribes, or by favouritism. The latter was a military medal (either of gold or silver) instituted by Sultan Abdul Hamid II. It is said that the stock is now exhausted, and that no more will be issued.

*War medals.*—The only war medal seen now is that for the Turco-Greek War of 1897. The ribbon for this consists of alternate narrow green and red stripes.

CIVIL ADMINISTRATION.

| | |
|---|---|
| Rais Beladiè ... ... | Mayor of a town. |
| Vali ... ... ... | Governor-General of a Province (*Vilayet*). |
| Mutessarif ... ... | Deputy Governor-General of a sub-province (*Sanjak*). |
| Kaimakam ... ... | Lieut.-Governor of a district (*Kazà*). |
| Mudir... ... ... | Head of a sub-district (*Nahié*). |
| Naib ... ... ... | Headman of village (*Köi*). |
| Bekji ... ... ... | A night watchman. |
| Colji ... ... ... | A watchman in employ of forestry department or of the Tobacco Company. |
| Gendarma ... ... | Mounted policeman. |

Zaptieh ... ... Mounted policeman (only used by villagers).
Koilar... ... ... Villager.
Religious persons—
Shaykh-ul-Islam ... Primate of all Mohammedans.
Dervish ... ... Member of a Mohammedan religious order.
Khoja ... ... Mohammedan teacher.
Said... ... ... A real or supposed descendant of Mohammed.
Hadji ... ... One who has made the pilgrimage to Mecca.
Mufti ... ... Doctor of Law.
Cadhi ... ... Judge.

## GENDARMERIE AND POLICE.

*Organization.*—The Turkish Gendarmerie was originally formed on the lines of the Macedonian Gendarmerie, which was forced on Turkey by the European Powers in 1904. In 1908, however, on the declaration of the Constitution, the foreign control ceased, but in 1909 the Turks extended this organization to the whole Empire (except Yemen and Hejaz), and retained the services of some of the British, French, and Italian officers, who remained as advisers without executive powers.

The gendarmerie is organized in regiments, with headquarters at the chief town of the *vilayet*, and containing battalions, companies, sections, varying in number and composition. In each unit there is a proportion of mounted gendarmes.

*Duties.*—The duties of the gendarmerie, who are scattered over the country in *karakols* or posts, of from one to two non-commissioned officers and three to eight men, are those of patrolling, correspondence, keeping roads open, escorts, &c. Summons are also served, recruits collected, and *Redifs* warned for service; in fact the gendarmes act as intermediaries between the Government and the people.

They are recruited from men who have either been called to the colours or have served in the army. The officers are taken from the army or are promoted from the ranks of the gendarmerie itself. Every gendarme must be unmarried, speak Turkish and, if illiterate, at least one of the other languages spoken in the *vilayet*.

*Zaptiehs.*—Side by side with the reformed gendarmerie there still exist many of the old *Zaptiehs*, both officers and men, who form the bulk of the gendarmerie regiments in Kurdistan and Mesopotamia. Their educational attainments are small, but on account of their intimate knowledge of the districts in which they usually serve all their lives, they are very useful as guides.

*Uniform.*—Single-breasted jacket of cornflower blue, with scarlet collar patches. Trousers of same colour and stuff as jacket. Black leather waist-belt with frog for bayonet, and black cross-belt with ammunition pouch behind.

*Armament.*—The gendarmerie is normally armed with the converted Mauser, though most of the Asiatic gendarmes still carry the Martini. Mounted gendarmes wear a sword instead of the bayonet.

N.B.—In time of war the gendarmerie is used for coast patrol work, defence of towns, isolated posts, &c., either as separate units or in conjunction with the military forces. Their early military training makes them a useful adjunct to the Turkish Army.

### *Police.*

*Organization.*—As distinct from the gendarmerie, who work chiefly in the country, the police are used in the large towns and centres of government. They are under the Minister of the Interior, and, except that the men are all old soldiers, are not a military force. The principal police official in each town is the *mudir* or director.

*Uniform.*—Single-breasted jacket of dark grey cloth, with scarlet patches on collar and cuffs; scarlet shoulder straps. Black trousers with red piping. Brown leather waist-belt and frog for sword.

*Armament.*—Policemen carry a short sword and a revolver. Officers carry an infantry sword.

### *Military Police.*

The military police are selected from the units in a garrison and wear their military uniform, with a prominent brass gorget inscribed *Kanun* (law), and are further distinguished by a yellow worsted aiguillette.

## Notes for Troops in regard to the Civil Population.

I.—Soldiers will come in contact with three different kinds of people:—Native Mohammedans, Native Christians, and Foreign Christians.

### Native Mohammedans—Men.

II.—(*a.*) Native Mohammedans are of two kinds—outside Constantinople they are all Turks; within Constantinople there are Turks and Mohammedans from other parts of the Empire, who are Kurds, Arabs, Circassians and Persians.

(*b.*) A country Turk of the villager class is to be known to a certain extent by his dress.

He wears as a rule a red fez, with a small coloured turban, a pair of very baggy bloomers of bluish cotton stuff, which are girt above the knee; a leather belt with a large pouch in front; white woollen stockings and large thick slippers.

(*c.*) A Constantinople Turk of the working class is difficult to recognise, except that all Turks wear red caps or fezes and only some Christians do.

(*d.*) The Kurds in Constantinople live mostly in the vicinity of the docks and quays. Some dress in shabby European clothes, and wear red caps, but a good many wear grey felt caps with a dark turban and brown baggy trousers reaching to the heels. Nearly all Kurds are very dark in complexion; they can mostly talk Turkish.

(*e.*) Arabs. There are very few Arabs in Constantinople; if a man wears a cloth over his head and a black rope twisted twice around it he is most likely an Arab. Very few Arabs can talk Turkish.

(*f.*) Circassians, of whom there are very few, are frequently quite fair in complexion, and almost all of them speak Turkish.

(*g.*) Persians, of whom there are not many, may be known by their black caps of felt. Persians are not Turkish subjects.

### Women Mohammedans.

Mohammedan village women wear gay-coloured clothes of red print, and veil themselves in white cloths, under which they wear a cap.

Mohammedan townswomen are generally dressed in black or mauve or some dark colour and wear black veils over their heads and faces.

### *Native Christians—Men.*

In the country around Constantinople on the European side there are Bulgarians and Greeks; dwelling in villages on the Asiatic side there are Greeks only.

In Constantinople there are both Greeks and Armenians:—

(*a.*) Bulgarians wear a black or grey cap and thick white woollen jackets and trousers.

(*b.*) Greek villagers on the coast usually wear black baggy bloomers, black stockings and a European hat, in the interior they wear a red fez, and sometimes a black turban.

(*c.*) Greek townsmen of all classes dress in European clothes and wear bowler, Trilby, or straw hats.

(*d.*) Armenians wear hats, red fezes, and sometimes black woollen caps; nearly all now wear European clothes.

### *Foreign Christians.*

These are Europeans; many are descendants of Europeans who came to Constantinople in the past. They are of all nations and wear European clothes.

### *Women Greeks.*

Greek women of the working class, in town or country, are dressed in black European clothes and wear a black cloth on their heads.

### *Clergy.*

Mohammedan clergy are always to be known by their white turbans, the white turban is only worn by clergymen, usually they wear baggy grey trousers and a dark blue gown, but sometimes wear villagers' clothes. A green turban denotes a man who has religious privileges.

Greek and Bulgarian clergy wear long hair and beards, the hair being tied in a knot at the back of their heads, a black gown and a hat like a top hat worn upside down.

Armenian clergy are dressed like Greek clergy save that the hat is replaced by a small round black cap.

## *Conduct towards Mohammedans.*

Soldiers must be careful to avoid doing anything contrary to the religious customs of the country.

A Mohammedan's headdress is sacred to him, and must not be touched even in fun.

A Mohammedan is forbidden to eat the flesh of pigs, therefore on no account offer a Mohammedan child any meat from your rations, as this might be misunderstood.

A Mohammedan's carpet is sacred ; if you have to go into a friendly house on some duty give the owner an opportunity of moving his prayer-carpet before going into a room.

On no account go into any mosque except on duty ; if billeted in a mosque roll up the carpets and put them away.

In town or country the following are regarded as sacred :—

>Trees which have rags tied to them,
>tombs,
>graveyards,
>deserted mosques,
>stones with inscriptions on them,
>fountains, and
>isolated clumps of trees on hill tops.

Soldiers should beware of defiling these objects by committing nuisances in their near neighbourhood, as the fact if noted may give rise to serious trouble long after.

Scraps of food other than bread should not be left about these places for the same reason.

Mohammedan women are veiled from all men except their husbands or near relations. On no account should any soldier take the least notice of any Mohammedan woman in town or country, either by staring at or speaking to her. This is a matter of great importance.

With regard to the whole civil Mohammedan population, soldiers should bear in mind that they will be regarded with considerable fear at first, and that any sudden act may provoke a panic owing to the Mohammedans expecting a massacre.

Good humour, firmness and quietness of manner are the

best way to dispel this fear, but familiarity should be avoided.

Bargaining, buying, and selling are frequent causes of misunderstanding, which gives rise to brawls spreading to panics. Soldiers should be on their guard in this matter.

All clergy, both Christian and Mohammedan, should be treated with due respect.

With regard to the Christian population, soldiers may expect to be welcomed, but they must beware of familiarity.

Soldiers are specially warned against drinking any native-made liquors; these are generally drugged and frequently poisonous.

In Constantinople itself soldiers must beware of the Europeans inhabiting the low class districts near the docks, cinematograph show keepers, grog-shop keepers, and the "hangers-on" of disorderly houses.

# APPENDICES.

## APPENDIX I.

### GLOSSARY OF MILITARY TERMS.

| | |
|---|---|
| Advanced guard | Pish-dar or Ileri karagul. |
| Ambush | Pussu. |
| Ammunition | Jebkhane. |
| ,, wagon | Jebkhane-arabasi. |
| Armistice | Mutareke. |
| Arms | Silah. |
| Army | Ordu. |
| ,, corps | Kol ordu. |
| Arsenal | Topkhane. |
| Artillery | Top-askerlar. |
| Artilleryman | Topji. |
| Assault | Hujum. |
| Axe | Balta. |
| Baggage | Eshia. |
| Bandolier | Fisheklik. |
| Barracks | Kishla. |
| Battalion | Tabur. |
| Battery (land fort) | Tabia. |
| ,, (field) | Batteria. |
| Bayonet | Sungu. |
| Brigade | Liva. |
| Bullet | Kurshun. |
| Calibre | Chap (S. B.) or kaliber (modern) |
| Camp | Ordugiah or Chadir yeri. |
| Cannonade | Top-ateshi. |
| Cartridge | Fishek. |
| Cavalry | Suwari-askeri. |
| Clip (Mauser cartridges) | Bir packet. |
| Company | Buluk. |
| Defeat | Bozghun. |
| Despatch | Tahrirat. |
| Division | Firka. |
| Driver | Arabaji. |
| Drum | Tranpeta. |
| Earthwork | Istikiam. |
| Enemy | Dushman. |
| Engineers | Istikiam alai. |
| ,, (civil) | ,, muhendiss. |
| ,, (mechanical) | ,, charkji. |

| | |
|---|---|
| Entrenchment | Meteriss. |
| Farrier | Nalband. |
| Field-gun | Siyar top. |
| Ford | Ghechid. |
| Fort | Tabia. |
| Fortification | Istikiamat. |
| Fortress | Kala. |
| Fuze (percussion) | Musademe tappa. |
| „ (time) | Sania tappa. |
| Governor (civil) | Vali. |
| Guardhouse | Karakol. |
| Gun | Top. |
| Gun carriage | Kundak. |
| Guncotton | Pambukbaruti. |
| Gun (Q.F.) | Siri atesh top. |
| Gunner | Topji. |
| Gunpowder | Barut. |
| „ (smokeless) | Domansiz barut. |
| Gunsmith | Tufenkji. |
| Hand-grenade | El khumbarassi. |
| Head-quarters | Merkez. |
| Hospital | Khastakhane. |
| Howitzer | Obuz. |
| Infantry | Piada askeri. |
| Lance | Mizrak or Karghi |
| Lancer | Mizrakli. |
| Limber (gun) | Topu toparlak. |
| „ (wagon) | Jebkhane toparlak. |
| Lines of communication | Khatt-i-mukhabere. |
| Lint | Yarabezi. |
| Load | Yuk. |
| Map | Kharita. |
| March | Asker-yurumessi. |
| Mortar | Hawan. |
| Musketry | Tufek atmassi-sanati. |
| Order | Emr. |
| Outpost | Ileri-karakol. |
| Peace | Sulh. |
| Picquet | Karakol. |
| Pontoon | Tombaz. |
| Pouch (ammunition) | Palaska. |
| Prisoner | Yessir or essir. |
| Private soldier | Nefer |
| Projectile | Mermi. |
| Rank | Rutbe. |
| Rear-guard | Dum-dar. |
| Reconnaissance | Istikshaf. |
| Redoubt | Tabia. |
| Regiment | Alai. |
| „ (infantry) | Piada alai. |

| | |
|---|---|
| Regiment (cavalry) | Suwari alai. |
| ,, (artillery) | Topji ,, |
| Reserve | Ihtiyat. |
| Rifle | Shishaneli Tufek or Tufek, Mauser Tufek, Martini Tufek |
| Rifleman | Nishanji. |
| Right. Left | Sagh. Sol. |
| Road | Yol. |
| Saddle | Eyer. |
| Scabbard | Kyn. |
| Section | Takim. |
| Sentry | Nubetji. |
| Sentry's challenge | Kim-dir-o or Kim-dir (who is that?). Answer—Kimse yok (it is no one), then bir Ingliz (an Englishman). |
| Shell (old spherical) | Kumbara. |
| ,, (common) | Takhrib danassi. |
| ,, (shrapnel) | Shrapnel dani. |
| ,, (chilled Palliser) | Kessir danassi. |
| ,, (steel) | Chelik ,, |
| Siege | Muhassara. |
| ,, gun | ,, top. |
| Squad | Takim. |
| Squadron | Suwari Buluk. |
| Strategy | Sevku-'l-jeysh. |
| Sword | Kilij. |
| Tactics | Tertibu-'l-jeysh. |
| Tent | Chadir. |
| Trail | Kuiruk. |
| Transport | Naklie. |
| Trumpet | Boru. |
| Uniform | Forma or Asker robassi. |
| Victory | Ghalebeh or Fatteh. |
| Wagon | Araba or Asker-arabasi. |
| Water carrier | Sakka. |
| Wheel | Tekerlek. |
| Wound dresser | Timarji. |

# APPENDIX II.

## TURKISH COINAGE, WEIGHTS AND MEASURES.

### GOLD COINAGE.

5, 2½, 1, ½ and ¼ lira pieces, of which the 1 and ½ lira are most seen. The lira (£T.) is worth nominally 100 gold piastre units, but there is no such actual coin as a gold piastre, and in practice the value of the lira in smaller currency is reckoned at a number of silver piastres varying according to locality. The usual number of silver piastres to a £T. is 108, but may be considerably more locally.

### SILVER COINAGE.

(i.) 1 mejidie of 20 piastres (grûsh) nominally, but actual number according to locality (about the size of a dollar).
(ii.) ½ mejidie of 10 piastres.
(iii.) 5 piastre piece, called a cherek or beshlik (about the size of a franc).
(iv.) 2 ,, ,,
(v.) 1 ,, ,, (grûsh).

The piastre is divided into 40 paras, a nominal division, as a piece of 5 paras is the smallest existing.
The following coins are made of alloy, called metallik:—

(i.) 100 para piece = 2½ piastres.
(ii.) 50 ,, = 1¼ ,,
(iii.) 10 ,, = ¼ piastre.
(iv.) 5 ,, = ⅛ ,,

There are also 10 and 20 para pieces of nickel.

### EQUIVALENTS IN BRITISH MONEY.

The £T. = 18s. 2d., the £ sterling being 112 piastres (nominal Government rate) or 118 to 120 for exchange when the £T. is 108.
The mejidie may be reckoned at about 3s. 4d., or Rs. 2.8, and the beshlik at 10d., or 10 annas.
There are certain variations, according to the rate of exchange of the day, but the local values of the piastre (referred to above) do not affect the value of the actual coins with respect to foreign money.

## Weights and Measures.

The following tables give the standard Turkish measures of weight, capacity, length:—

|  | Turkish, equal to | English, equal to. |
|---|---|---|
| *Weights.* | | |
| 1 kerat | ... | 3·09537 grains. |
| 16 kerats | 1 dirhem | 49·40717 ,, |
| 1½ dirhems | 1 miskal | 74·245 ,, |
| 176 ,, | 1 lodra | 1·2141 lb. ⎫ Avoirdupois. |
| 400 ,, | 1 oke | 2·832 ,, ⎬ |
| 44 okes or 100 lodras | 1 kantar | 124·6 ,, ⎪ |
| 4 kantars or 400 lodras | 1 cheki | 498·4 ,, ⎭ |
| 18 ,, or 792 okes. | 1 tonnellatta | 1 ton. |
| *Measures.* | | |
| Capacity— | | |
| 1 kutu | ... | 1·01795 gallon. |
| 8 kutus | 1 kile | 1·618 bushel. |
| 8·1446 kiles | ... | 1 quarter. |
| Length— | | |
| Endazé, measure for cotton stuffs, carpets, &c.— | | |
| 1 jera | ... | 1·62 inch. |
| 2 jeras | 1 rup | 3·24 inches. |
| 8 rups | 1 endazé (pik) | 25·91 ,, |
| Arshin, measure for silks and woollen stuffs— | | |
| 1 jera | ... | 1·674 inch. |
| 2 jeras | 1 rup | 3·348 inches. |
| 8 rups | 1 arshin (pik) | 26·772 ,, |
| Zira, measure for land— | | |
| 1 nokta | ... | 0·0868 inch. |
| 12 ,, | 1 khat | 0·1036 ,, |
| 12 khats | 1 parmrk | 1·24 ,, |
| 14 parmaks | 1 zira | 29·84 inches. |
| Superficial— | | |
| 1,600 square ziras | 1 donum | 1,099·373 sq. yards. |
| 4·4024 donums | ... | 1 acre. |

## Notes.

The oke is the ordinary standard weight for solids and liquids.
180 okes = 1 cheki or load, or 176 okes used for wood measure.
Liquid.—2¼ okes = 1,000 drams = 1 binlik or demijohn, wicker-covered large bottles for wine and raki.
The size of the kile varies throughout the country.
2 kutu (box used to measure animal's food) = 1 shinik.
3 French litres are equal to 1 Constantinople kile, which is rather over 2½ quarts.
1 parmak, or finger, is roughly used as equal to an inch.
1 karish, or span of the outspread fingers, is used to indicate about 8 inches. A ford is said to be 4 karish (spans), i.e., about 3 feet.
A kulaj means the width of chest and the outspread arms, and is rather less than a fathom.
The pik is a measure varying according to material measured.
Land is measured by square piks and donums, the latter being usually taken at about ¼ acre.

### Distance and Time.

Distance is measured in Turkey by hours.
One hour is reckoned as about 3 miles, or as the distance a pedestrian will cover in that time.
The Moslem day is reckoned from sunset to sunset and is divided into 24 hours, which are counted as twice twelve. Sunset is reckoned at 12 o'clock and is the fixed reckoning for each day; 12 hours after sunset is again 12 o'clock.
The Moslem calendar begins with 16th July, in the year 622 A.D., this being the date of the Hegira, or flight of Mohammed from Mecca to Medina. The Moslem year is a purely lunar year of 12 months. Each of the odd-numbered months contain 29 days, each of the even-numbered months 30 days. There are thus 354 days in the year, or 355 in leap year, 11 of which occur in each cycle of 30 years. In the course of 33 years each month makes a complete circuit of the seasons. On 25th February, 1906, began the year 1324 of the Hegira, but the official or financial year is now reckoned 2 years earlier, consequently the Turkish year, 1331, corresponds to our 1915, although the actual year of the Hegira is 1333.

## APPENDIX III.

### TURKISH VOCABULARY AND PHRASES.

*Pronunciation—*

All consonants as in English. It must be noted, however, that "r" must never be allowed to affect the vowel which it follows, and must be pronounced as in Italian.

All the vowels are to be pronounced as in German—ö = French *eu*; ü = French *u*.

Long vowels are marked with an accent.

Gh is to be pronounced like "ch" in loch, with a "g" sound instead of "c."

#### TOPOGRAPHICAL.

*Countries and places.*

| | |
|---|---|
| Austria | Nemsé. |
| Austrian | Nemseli. |
| England | Inghilterra. |
| Englishman | Ingliz. |
| Egypt | Misr. |
| France | Fransa. |
| Frenchman | Fransiz. |
| Germany | Alemania. |
| German | Aleman. |
| Greece | Yunán. |
| Greek | Yunanli. |
| Montenegro | Karadagh. |
| Montenegrin | Karadaghli. |
| Persia | Ajam. |
| Russia | Russia, Moskov. |
| Russian | Moskovli. |
| Turkey | Memleket-i-Osmaniya, Turkia |
| Turk | Osmanli. |
| Constantinople | Stambul. |
| Smyrna | Izmir. |
| Alexandretta | Iskanderun |
| Aleppo | Haleb. |
| Tripoli | Trablus. |
| Damascus | Shám. |
| Jerusalem | Kudus. |
| Cyprus | Kubrus. |
| Beersheba | Bir es Saba. |
| Mytilene | Midilli. |

| | |
|---|---|
| Black Sea | Kara Deniz. |
| Marmora | Mermer Denizi |
| Costanza | Kustenji. |
| Rhodes | Rodos. |

*Topographical.*

| | |
|---|---|
| rock | kaya. |
| stone | tásh. |
| sea | deniz. |
| lake | gyöl. |
| fountain | cheshmé. |
| river | irmak, su. |
| well | kuyu. |
| stream | chai, akar su |
| mountain | dágh. |
| pass | boghaz. |
| neck of pass | bel. |
| saltpan | tuzla. |
| hill | tepé. |
| plain | ova. |
| field | tarla. |
| forest | orman. |
| tree | aghách. |
| farm | chiftlik. |
| valley | dere. |
| headland | burun. |
| marsh | balchik, batak |
| castle | hissár. |
| town | shéhir, kassaba. |
| village | kiöi. |
| place | yer. |
| made road | shossé yolu. |
| high road | jáddé. |
| wheel traffic road | araba yolu. |
| road | yol. |
| bridge | kyöprü. |
| ford | gechid. |
| port | liman. |
| quay | rihtim. |
| ferry | gechid yeri. |
| camp | karar-gyah. |
| church | kilisé. |
| mosque | jami. |
| barracks | kishla. |
| tent | chadir. |
| school | mekteb. |
| railway station | istasion. |
| hospital | hasta-háné. |

| | | |
|---|---|---|
| restaurant | ... | locanta. |
| post office | ... | posta-háné. |
| telegraph office | ... | telegráf-háné |
| shrine | ... | turbé. |
| monastery (dervishes) | ... | tekke. |
| library | ... | kutub-háné. |
| baths | ... | hammám. |
| shop | ... | dükyán. |
| ruins | ... | veiren. |
| province | ... | vilayet. |
| sub-province | ... | sanjak. |
| district | ... | kaza. |
| sub-district | ... | nahié. |
| governor's office | ... | konak, seray. |

## ANIMALS, TRANSPORT, &c.

| | | |
|---|---|---|
| horse | ... | át. |
| mare | ... | kisrak. |
| horseshoe | ... | na'al. |
| blacksmith | ... | demirji, na'alband (special smith for shoeing horses). |
| mule | ... | katir. |
| muleteer | ... | katirji. |
| donkey | ... | merkeb, eshek. |
| ox | ... | öküz. |
| cow | ... | inek. |
| bull | ... | bogha. |
| calf | ... | dana. |
| buffalo | ... | manda. |
| sheep | ... | kuyún. |
| lamb | ... | kúzu. |
| goat | ... | kechi. |
| dog | ... | kyöpek. |
| cat | ... | kedi. |
| flea | ... | piré. |
| bug | ... | takhta-biti. |
| louse | ... | bit. |
| hay | ... | kuru ot. |
| straw (chopped) | ... | saman. |
| oats | ... | yulaf. |
| barley | ... | arpa (arpa-saman = horses feed of barley and chopped straw). |
| saddle | ... | eyer. |
| bridle | ... | bashlik. |
| cart | ... | araba. |
| lorry | ... | vurghun arabasi. |
| ammunition wagon | ... | jebhané-arabasi |
| baggage | ... | eshya |
| railway | ... | demir yolú, shemen-de-fer |

| | | | | |
|---|---|---|---|---|
| rail | ... | ... | ... | raï |
| truck | ... | ... | ... | vagon. |
| engine | ... | ... | ... | mákina |
| steamer | ... | ... | ... | vápor |
| boat | ... | ... | ... | sandal |
| oar | ... | ... | ... | kürek |
| raft | ... | ... | ... | sál |
| sails | ... | ... | ... | yelkenler |
| mast | ... | ... | ... | direk |

### WEATHER, TIMES AND SEASONS.

| | | | | |
|---|---|---|---|---|
| weather | ... | ... | ... | hava (very important word if bad (fana) it means that the neighbourhood is feverish) |
| storm | ... | ... | ... | fortúna |
| sun | ... | ... | ... | günésh |
| moon | ... | ... | ... | ái |
| rain | ... | ... | ... | yaghmúr |
| snow | ... | ... | ... | kar |
| hail | ... | ... | ... | dolu |
| ice | ... | ... | ... | buz |
| frost | ... | ... | ... | kira |
| thaw | ... | ... | ... | karlarin erimesi |
| fog | ... | ... | ... | dumán |
| wind | ... | ... | ... | ruzgyar |
| cloud | ... | ... | ... | bulút |
| thunder | ... | ... | ... | } gyök gyürlemesi |
| thunderstorm | ... | ... | ... | } gyök gyüruldüsü |
| time | ... | ... | ... | vakit |
| year | ... | ... | ... | yil, sené |
| spring | ... | ... | ... | ilk bahár |
| summer | ... | ... | ... | yáz |
| autumn | ... | ... | ... | son bahár. |
| winter | ... | ... | ... | kísh. |
| month | ... | ... | ... | ái. |
| week | ... | ... | ... | hafta. |
| day | ... | ... | ... | gyün. |
| hour | ... | ... | ... | sa'at (important as marching a league in distance). |
| minute | ... | ... | ... | dakíka. |
| morning | ... | ... | ... | sabáh. |
| noon | ... | ... | ... | ölén. |
| afternoon | ... | ... | ... | ikindi |
| evening | ... | ... | ... | akhshám. |
| night | ... | ... | ... | géjé. |
| sunset | ... | ... | ... | ghurúb. |
| Sunday | ... | ... | ... | Bázár-günü. |
| Monday | ... | ... | ... | Bázár-ertesi. |
| Tuesday | ... | ... | ... | Sáli-günü. |
| Wednesday | ... | ... | ... | Chár-shamba. |

| | | |
|---|---|---|
| Thursday | ... | Pershembé. |
| Friday | ... | Jum'a. |
| Saturday | ... | Jum'a-ertesi. |

## Hours of prayer.

| | |
|---|---|
| prayer | namáz. |
| five prayers in the day— | |
| 1 sunrise | sabáh namázi. |
| 2 midday | ölen namázi. |
| 3 2.30 p.m. | ikindi namázi. |
| 4 sunset | aksham namázi. |
| 5 two hours after sunset | yatsi namázi. |
| January | Kyánún-i-sáni. |
| February | Shubát. |
| March | Mart. |
| April | Nisán. |
| May | Mais. |
| June | Hazirán. |
| July | Temmuz. |
| August | Agystos. |
| September | Eylúl. |
| October | Teshrín-i-evvel. |
| November | Teshrín-i-sáni. |
| December | Kyánún-i-evvel. |
| Easter | Paskaliya. |

## NUMERALS, &c.

| | | | |
|---|---|---|---|
| 1 | bir. | 90 | doksan. |
| 2 | iki. | 100 | yüz. |
| 3 | üch. | 101 | yüz bir. |
| 4 | dört. | 1,000 | bin. |
| 5 | besh. | | |
| 6 | alti. | I | ben. |
| 7 | yedi. | thou | sen. |
| 8 | sekiz. | he | o. |
| 9 | dokuz. | we | biz. |
| 10 | on. | you | siz. |
| 11 | on-bir. | they | onlar. |
| 12 | on-iki. | | |
| 13 | on-üch. | $\frac{1}{2}$ | yari. |
| 14 | on-dört. | and a half | buchuk. |
| 15 | on-besh. | | (e.g., bir buchuk, 1½.) |
| 20 | yirmi. | $\frac{1}{4}$ | cheirek. |
| 21 | yirmi bir. | first | birinji. |
| 22 | yirmi iki. | second | ikinji. |
| 30 | otuz. | third | üchünji. |
| 40 | kirk. | fourth | dördunju. |
| 50 | elli. | fifth | beshinji. |
| 60 | altmish. | sixth | altinji. |
| 70 | yetmish. | once | bir defa. |
| 80 | seksen. | twice | iki defa. |

## Domestic, &c.

| | |
|---|---|
| house | ev. |
| room | oda. |
| staircase | merdiven. |
| mill | deghürmen. |
| door | kapu. |
| kitchen | mutbakh. |
| stable | áhur. |
| bed | düshek, yatak. |
| carpet | kilim, háli. |
| oven | furun. |
| firewood | odun. |
| fireplace | oják. |
| coal | kyömür. |
| lamp | lamba. |
| matches | kibrít. |
| thing | shéi. |
| window | penjeré. |
| roof | dám. |
| blanket | yorgan. |
| soap | sábún. |
| towel | havlu, peshkir. |
| chair | sandalié. |
| table | massa. |
| kettle | güyün. |
| saucepan | tenjeré. |
| cap | kálpak. |
| pen | kálem. |
| ink | murekkeb. |
| man | ádem. |
| woman | kári. |
| boy | chojuk. |
| girl | kiz. |
| children and family | } choluk-chojuk. |
| knee | diz. |
| foot | ayak. |
| hand | el. |
| leg | bajak. |
| neck | boyun. |
| arm | kol. |
| shoulder | omuz. |
| stomach | midé. |
| screw | vidé. |
| water carrier | sakka. |
| secretary | kyátib. |
| servant | hizmetji, ushák. |
| bucket | kogha. |
| water skin | korba. |
| bottle | shishé. |

| | |
|---|---|
| cork | tapa. |
| rope | } ip, urghan. |
| cord | |
| spade | bel. |
| shovel | kyürek. |
| pick-axe | kázma. |
| plough | sabán. |
| hammer | chekij, tokmák |
| nail | chivi. |
| saw | testere. |
| chisel | kalem. |
| pincers | kerbeten. |
| sack | chewel, torba. |
| leather | meshín. |
| top-boot | chizma |
| boot | ayak-kabu, bottina. |
| shoe | pápush. |
| whip | kámchi. |
| spur | mahmuz |
| cotton | pamuk. |
| needle | iné. |
| scissors | makáss. |
| thimble | yüksük. |
| button | düimé. |
| lace (boot) | cordela. |
| book | kitáb. |
| paper | kyágid. |
| letter | mektüb. |

## Food and drink.

| | |
|---|---|
| breakfast | kahvalti. |
| food | yemek. |
| water | su. |
| bread | ekmek. |
| flour | un. |
| meat | et. |
| mutton | kuyún eti. |
| kid | oghlak eti. |
| fish | balik. |
| egg | yumurtah. |
| milk | sud. |
| sour milk | yaghurt. |
| butter | teré yághi. |
| melted butter | süzülmish yágh. |
| cheese | penir. |
| salt | túz. |
| sugar | skeker. |
| soup | chorba. |
| boiled rice | pilaf. |

| | |
|---|---|
| duck | ördek |
| goose | kaz. |
| chicken | pilij. |
| potato | patátes. |
| mealies | misir-boghdái. |
| rice | pirinj. |
| beans | fasulia, bakla. |
| vegetables | sebzevát. |
| jam | tatli. |
| cake | börek. |
| beer | 'bira. |
| wine | sharáb. |
| spirits | müskerát. |
| tea | chái. |
| coffee | kahvé. |
| water | su. |
| bottle | shishé. |
| glass | kadeh. |
| cup | filján. |
| kettle | kazghán, kázan. |
| brazier | manghál. |
| tobacco | tütün. |

## ADJECTIVES.

| | |
|---|---|
| all | hepsi. |
| angry | darghín. |
| bad | fená, küttür. |
| beautiful | gyüzel. |
| big | büyük. |
| biggest | en büyük. |
| bitter | áji. |
| black | kara. |
| blue | mavi. |
| brave | jesúr. |
| broad | ghenish. |
| brown | esmer. |
| cheap | ujuz. |
| cheerful | shen. |
| clean | temiz. |
| cold | so'uk. |
| crooked | éiri. |
| damp | nemlak. |
| dark | karanlik. |
| dear | aziz. |
| dear (price) | pahali. |
| deep | derin. |
| difficult | güch. |
| dirty | pis. |

| | |
|---|---|
| disobedient | itá'atsiz. |
| dry | kuru. |
| easy | kolái. |
| empty | bosh. |
| every | her. |
| far | uzak. |
| flat | duz |
| friendly | dostané. |
| full | dolu. |
| good | iyi. |
| [better] best | en iyi, en alá. |
| green | yeshil. |
| grey | kir |
| hard and difficult | sert. |
| heavy | aghir. |
| high | yüksek. |
| hostile | dushman. |
| hungry | áj. |
| ignorant | jehil. |
| impudent | kustákh. |
| large | büyük. |
| left | sol tarafda. |
| light | hafíf. |
| light (colour) | achik. |
| little | küchuk. |
| long | uzun. |
| low | álchak. |
| narrow | dar. |
| near | yakin. |
| new | yeni. |
| none | hich bir. |
| obedient | ita'atlu. |
| obstinate | inadji. |
| old | eski. |
| open | áchik. |
| poor | fukara. |
| quick | chabúk. |
| ready | házir. |
| red | kirmizi. |
| rich | zengin. |
| right | hakk-li. |
| right (direction) | sagh tarafda. |
| round | yuvarlak. |
| short | kisa. |
| sick | hasta. |
| skilful | hünerli. |
| small | küchik. |
| smooth | duz. |
| soft | yumushak. |
| solid | muhkyem. |

| | | | | |
|---|---|---|---|---|
| straight | ... | ... | ... | doghru. |
| s upid | ... | ... | ... | shashkin. |
| suitable | ... | ... | ... | münásib. |
| sweet | ... | ... | .. | tatli. |
| thick | ... | ... | ... | kalín. |
| thin | ... | ... | ... | injé. |
| timid | ... | ... | ... | korkak. |
| tired | ... | ... | ... | yorghún. |
| treacherous | ... | ... | ... | ghaddár. |
| true | ... | ... | ... | gyerchek, doghru. |
| unjust | ... | ... | ... | insafsiz. |
| unlucky | ... | ... | ... | bakhtsiz. |
| warm | ... | ... | ... | siják. |
| weak | ... | ... | ... | zá'if. |
| white | ... | ... | ... | ák, beyaz. |
| whole | ... | ... | ... | temàm, bitun. |
| wide | ... | ... | ... | ghenish. |
| yellow | ... | ... | ... | sári. |
| young | ... | ... | ... | genj. |

## VERBS.

The following are all given in the positive imperative tense, except when otherwise stated. For negative imperative, add the word má :—

| | | | | |
|---|---|---|---|---|
| I can | ... | ... | ... | bilirem. |
| accompany | ... | ... | ... | beraber git. |
| answer | ... | ... | ... | jeváb ver. |
| ask | ... | ... | ... | sor. |
| begin | ... | ... | ... | bashla. |
| believe | .. | ... | ... | inan. |
| bleed | ... | ... | ... | kánayur. |
| break | ... | ... | ... | kir. |
| broken | ... | ... | ... | kirik. |
| bring | ... | ... | ... | getir |
| build | ... | ... | ... | yap. |
| buy | ... | ... | ... | sátin-al. |
| burn | ... | ... | ... | yan. |
| bury | ... | ... | ... | defn-et, gyumm |
| call | ... | ... | ... | chagir. |
| carry | ... | ... | ... | táshi. |
| catch | ... | ... | ... | tut. |
| clean | ... | ... | ... | temizle |
| come | ... | ... | ... | gel |
| cook | ... | ... | ... | pishir. |
| deceive | ... | ... | ... | aldat. |
| defend | ... | ... | ... | muhafezé-et. |
| describe | .. | ... | ... | ta'ríf-et. |

| | |
|---|---|
| destroy | yik. |
| die | ül. |
| dig | kaz. |
| disappear | ghaib-ol. |
| discover | bul. |
| do | yap. |
| doubt | shubhé-et. |
| draw (map, &c.) | ressim-et. |
| dress | giyindir. |
| drink | ich. |
| dry | kurut. |
| eat | ye. |
| end (trans.) | bïtir. |
| err | hatá et. |
| examine | imtihán et. |
| excuse | afv et. |
| fall | düsh. |
| fear | kork. |
| fetch | gidup-getir. |
| fill | doldur. |
| find | bul. |
| flee | kách. |
| follow | arkasina-dush |
| fortify | istikyám et. |
| frighten | korkut. |
| get | al, ghetir. |
| give | ver. |
| go | git. |
| go in | gir. |
| go out | dishári chik. |
| guide | yol gyüster. |
| halt | éilen, dur. |
| hang up | as. |
| hear | ishit. |
| heat | issit. |
| help | yardim et. |
| hide | saklá. |
| hinder | máni ol. |
| hold | tut. |
| hold out | dayan. |
| hope | umíd et. |
| hurry | ajélé et. |
| inform | haber ver. |
| keep | sakla. |
| kill | üldür. |
| know | bil. |
| lay | kur. |
| learn | ûghren |
| lead | öne dush |
| leave | brák. |

| | | | | |
|---|---|---|---|---|
| lie | ... | ... | ... | yát. |
| lie (untruth) | ... | ... | ... | yalar, söilé. |
| listen | ... | ... | ... | dinlé. |
| live (*i.e.*, dwell) | | ... | ... | otur. |
| load | ... | ... | ... | yuklé. |
| lock | ... | ... | ... | kilitlé. |
| look at | ... | ... | ... | bák. |
| lose | ... | ... | ... | gháib et. |
| make | ... | ... | ... | yap. |
| meet | ... | ... | ... | rást gel. |
| mend | ... | ... | ... | tamir et. |
| open | ... | ... | ... | âch. |
| order | ... | ... | ... | emr-et. |
| pay | ... | ... | ... | ödé. |
| play | ... | ... | ... | oina. |
| plunder | ... | ... | ... | yaghmá et |
| pour out | ... | ... | ... | dük. |
| promise | ... | ... | ... | söz vér. |
| punish | ... | ... | ... | terbié et. |
| pursue | ... | ... | ... | ta'kíb et. |
| read | ... | ... | ... | oku. |
| remain | ... | ... | ... | kál. |
| rest | ... | ... | ... | dinlen. |
| return | ... | ... | ... | gheri-dön. |
| ride | ... | ... | ... | bin. |
| run | ... | ... | ... | kósh. |
| saddle | ... | ... | ... | eyyerlé. |
| sally out | | ... | ... | ilerile. |
| say | ... | ... | ... | söilé. |
| see | ... | ... | ... | gyür. |
| seek | ... | ... | ... | ará. |
| seize | ... | ... | ... | káp. |
| sell | ... | ... | ... | sát. |
| send | ... | ... | ... | gyünder. |
| shoe | ... | ... | ... | na 'alla. |
| shoot | ... | ... | ... | át |
| show | ... | ... | ... | gyüster. |
| shut | ... | ... | ... | kapá. |
| silent, to be | ... | ... | ... | suss. |
| sit | ... | ... | ... | otur [sit down = buyurun!] |
| slaughter | ... | ... | ... | kess. |
| sleep | ... | ... | ... | uyu |
| smoke | ... | ... | ... | tütün ich. |
| speak | ... | ... | ... | söilé. |
| stand | ... | ... | ... | dur. |
| strike | ... | ... | ... | vúr. |
| surrender | ... | ... | ... | teslim ol. |
| swim | ... | ... | ... | yüz. |
| take | ... | ... | ... | ál. |
| teach | ... | ... | ... | üghret. |

| | |
|---|---|
| tell | habar ver. |
| thank | teshekkür |
| think | düshün. |
| thirst | súsá. |
| threaten | kurkut. |
| touch | dokun. |
| translate | terjumé et |
| try | chálish. |
| turn back | geri dün. |
| undress oneself | soyun. |
| wait | beklé. |
| wake | uyandir. |
| wake up | uyan. |
| wander | dolash. |
| wash | yiká. |
| wash oneself | yikán. |
| win | kazán. |
| wish | isté. |
| work | ishé. |
| write | yáz. |

ADVERBS.

| | |
|---|---|
| here | burádé. |
| there | orádé. |
| where | neredé. |
| whither | nereyé. |
| hither | burayó. |
| thither | orayó. |
| whence | nereden. |
| nowhere | hich bir yerdé. |
| everywhere | her yerdé. |
| above | yukari. |
| below | altenda. |
| outside | dishari. |
| inside | icheri. |
| behind | ard [behind me=ardimda]. |
| in front | ileri [go before us=bizden ileri git]. |
| near | yakin. |
| far | uzak. |
| when | ne vakit. |
| then | ol vakit. |
| now | shimdi. |
| at once | derhál. |
| never | hich bir wakit. |
| always | dá'ima. |
| often | chok vakitlar. |
| rarely | nádir. |
| suddenly | apansiz. |
| already | dahá, henüz. |

| | | | | |
|---|---|---|---|---|
| still | ... | ... | ... | dahá. |
| not yet | ... | ... | ... | dahá—yok or deyil. |
| soon | ... | ... | ... | } chabúk. |
| quickly | ... | ... | ... | |
| early | ... | ... | ... | erken. |
| late | ... | ... | ... | gech. |
| to-day | ... | ... | ... | bu gyün. |
| yesterday | ... | ... | ... | dün. |
| to-morrow | ... | ... | ... | yarin. |
| much | ... | ... | ... | chok. |
| more | ... | ... | ... | ziádé. |
| little | ... | ... | ... | az. |
| at least | ... | ... | ... | hich olmaz issé. |
| how much | ... | ... | ... | kach. |
| so much | ... | ... | ... | ol kadar. |
| accidentally | ... | ... | ... | kazâ'ar, rasst ghelé. |
| certainly | ... | ... | ... | el-betté. |
| not at all | ... | ... | ... | haïr, yok. |
| enough | ... | ... | ... | kyafi. |
| very | ... | ... | ... | pek, chok. |

PREPOSITIONS. IN TURKISH POSTPOSITIONS PLACED AFTER THE WORD IN QUESTION AND USUALLY JOINED ON TO IT.

| | | | | |
|---|---|---|---|---|
| after | ... | ... | ... | -dan sora. |
| at | ... | ... | ... | -da. |
| between | ... | ... | ... | arasinda. |
| before | ... | ... | ... | -dan evvel. |
| opposite | ... | ... | ... | karshu. |
| behind | ... | ... | ... | arkasinda. |
| except | ... | ... | ... | -dan bashka. |
| from | ... | ... | ... | -dan. |
| in | ... | ... | ... | -da. |
| into | ... | ... | ... | ichiné. |
| on | ... | ... | ... | üzerinda. |
| out of | ... | ... | ... | -dan. |
| owing to, because of | ... | | | ichün, sebebinden. |
| since | ... | ... | ... | dan beri. |
| through | ... | ... | ... | ichindan. |
| to | ... | ... | ... | -e, -ye. |
| towards | ... | ... | ... | -ye dogru. |
| till | ... | ... | ... | -ye kadar. |
| under | ... | ... | ... | altinda. |
| with | ... | ... | ... | -ilé. |
| without | ... | ... | ... | -siz. |
| by and for | ... | ... | ... | -ichün. |

CONJUNCTIONS.

| | | | | |
|---|---|---|---|---|
| and | ... | ... | ... | vé. |
| but | ... | ... | ... | lakin. |

| | | | | | |
|---|---|---|---|---|---|
| if | ... | ... | ... | ... | eger. |
| that | ... | ... | ... | ... | ki. |
| only | ... | ... | ... | ... | yaliniz. |
| or... | ... | ... | ... | ... | yakhud. |
| still | ... | ... | ... | ... | heutiz. |
| why | ... | ... | ... | ... | nichtin. |
| because | ... | ... | ... | ... | bunun ichtin. |
| yes | ... | ... | ... | ... | evvet. |
| no | ... | ... | ... | ... | haïr. |

## QUESTIONS AND ANSWERS.

### 1. Time and place.

| | |
|---|---|
| Where is --? | Nérédé dir? |
| Where are you going? | Néréyé gidiyorsiniz? |
| Where have you come from? | Nereden geliyürsiniz? |
| Turn to the right (left) | Sàgh (sol) tarafa dön! |
| Stand still there | Orade dur. |
| Give me water | Bana su ver! |
| Here is water and brandy | Ishté su ve konyak. |
| Give me a bandage | Bana sarghi ver! |
| Go to the doctor and tell him to come at once | Hekimi chaghir—chábuk gelsin! |
| Take this medicine | Bu ilaji ál. |
| Take this man to hospital | Bu ádemi hastabanéye gyötur. |

### Weather and Time.

| | |
|---|---|
| What will the weather be to-day? | Bu gyüki hava né durlu olajak? |
| Very fine | Pek gyüzel. |
| Bad, cloudy, foggy weather | Fena, bulanik, tumanli. |
| It is snowing on the mountains. | Daghi-da kár yaghiyor! |
| What is the time? | Sá'at kach dir? |

### General.

| | |
|---|---|
| Do you know English? | Inglizija bilürmisiniz? |
| Speak slowly | Yawásh söilé! |
| There is a fire! | Yangin vár! |
| Impossible | Olmaz! |
| Please, come in! sit down, &c | Buyurun! |
| God grant it! | Allah versin! |
| Good morning, sir | Sabahiniz hair olsún, efendim |
| How is your honourable health? | Mizaj-i sherifiniz nasil dir? |
| It is true | Doghru dir. |
| What are your wishes? | Arzunuz né-dir. |

| | |
|---|---|
| Thank God, I am well | Hamd olsun iyi-yim. |
| You are welcome | Hosh geldün. |
| Please! | Lutfen, Rija Iderim. |
| What news is there? | Ne habar var? |
| There is no news | Habar yok! |
| How do you know? | Nasl bilursiniz? |
| It is false | Yalan dir. |
| I am glad | Memnun-im. |
| I am sorry | Te'essuf iderim. |
| Possible | Mümkin. |
| Impossible | Mumkin diyil. |
| Rain threatens | Yagmur yagajakmish |
| It is moonlight | Maitab var. |
| How old are you? | Kach yashinda siniz? |
| I must go | Gitmeli-yim. |
| Is he at home? | Evdé mi dir? |
| Who is it? | Kim dir? |
| Let him enter! | Gelsnu icheri! |
| Does the water boil? | Su kainayor-mi? |
| Wait for me | Beni beklé. |
| Come with me | Benim ilé gel. |
| Go away | Haidé git! chikiniz! |
| How far is it? | Né kadar uzak dir? |
| It is not far | Uzak deyil dir. |
| Two hours' distance | Iki sa'at yol. |
| When will he come? | Ne vakit geliyor. |
| At what o'clock? | Sa'at kach-da? |
| At six o'clock | Sa'at alti-da. |
| In the morning | Sabah-da. |
| At noon | Oilenda. |
| In the evening | Akhsham-ustu. |

*The road.*

| | |
|---|---|
| Where does this road go? | Bu yol nereye chikar? |
| Does this road go to —? | — ye yol bú-mú? |
| Which is the shortest way? | — ye en kissa yol hanghisi dir? |
| Straight on | Doghru. |
| Is there danger on this road? | Bu yolda tehliké var mi? |
| It is a very good road | Bu pek iyi yol dir. |
| How many hours is it to -?| — ye kach sá'at yol dir? |
| Take me to — | Beni — ye gyötur! |

*A village or town.*

| | |
|---|---|
| What is this place called? | Burasiné né der ler? |
| How many houses in this village? | Bu kyöi kach haneli-dir? |
| Where is the post? | Posta khané neredé dir? |

| | |
|---|---|
| Show me the telegraph office | Telegraf-hané gyöster! |
| Is there a telephone office here? | Telefon burada var-mi? |
| Where is the inn? | Han neredé dir? |
| We are going to stay the night here. | Bu akhsham búrada kalajayiz |

## At a River.

| | |
|---|---|
| What is this river called? | Bu suye né derler? |
| How deep is the river? | Bu su né kadar derin dir? |
| Where is the nearest bridge? | En yakin kyöprü neredé dir? |
| Take me there | Beni orayé gyötur! |
| Show me the nearest ferry | En yakin gechidyeri bana gyöster! |
| Get hold of a boat (canoe) | Bir kaïk bul! |
| Is there a raft here? | Kelek var mi? |
| Is the current strong? | Ákindi küvvetli mi dir? |
| Where is the easiest place to swim across? | Yuzerek gechmek ichün en kolai yer neresi dir? |
| Take us across | Bizi karshu-ye gechir! |
| You will be rewarded | Size bakhshish verejeyiz. |
| You must go in front of me | Ileri gitmeli siniz! |
| What place lies on the other side? | Karshu-da ne kyöi var! |
| Is it far to the mouth? | Irmak (chaï) aghzi uzak mi dir? |

## A Mountain or Hill.

| | |
|---|---|
| What is this big mountain called? | Bu büyük dághe né derler? |
| How high is the mountain? | Bu dágh né kadar yüksek dir? |
| What is the easiest way up the hill? | Tepe-ye chikmak ichün en kolai yol hanghisi dir |
| Is it very steep? | Pek dik mi dir? |
| Is it dangerous? | Tehlikeli mi dir? |
| Can one get up on horseback? | Hayvan yoli var mi? |
| Can the guns be got up? | Toplar ichün yol var mi? |
| Yes, but they cannot be got down on the other side. | Evvet, lakin öte inishda yol yokdir? |
| Are there several ways down? | Öté inishda kach yol var? |

## A Forest.

| | |
|---|---|
| How big is the forest? | Ormán ne kadar büyük dir? |
| How wide is it? | Né kadar enli dir? |
| Where does the road go through the forest? | Ormánin yoli nerede dir? |
| Can caravans get through the forest? | Bu ormanda kerwan yoli vár? |
| Yes, but I don't think one can get through with guns. | Evvet, lákin toplar ichün yol yok dir. |

## A Railway Station.

| | |
|---|---|
| Is it far to the railway? | Demir yol uzak mi dir? |
| Only half-an-hour | Yárim sáat. |
| When does the train arrive? | Tren ne vakit geliyor? |
| When does the train go to —? | Tren ne vakit—ye gidiyor? |
| Where is the next train coming from? | Soraki tren nereden geliyor? |
| Stop the train! | Treni durdur. |
| Get me a porter! | Hamál getir! |

## Inquiry about Troops.

| | |
|---|---|
| Have you seen our troops? | Bizim askerleri györdünüzmü? |
| Do you know where the Turkish troops are? | Osmanli askerleri neredé dirler bilür mi siniz? |
| Yes, I saw them by the wood | Evvet, oulari ormánda györdüm. |
| What sort of troops and how many are they? | Né dorlu dir? Kach var? |
| Five thousand, with cavalry and guns. | Besh bin, átli ve toplar. |
| Since when are they there? | Ne zamandenberi orada buluniyorlar? |
| In which direction have they marched? | Hangi tarafa gitdilar? |
| Where is an officer? | Zábit nerede dir? |
| Take me to the colonel | Mir alái ye beni gyötur. |
| I have a letter from our general. | Amirimizdan bir mektüb var. |

## Food and Drink.

| | |
|---|---|
| Where can I get food? | Yemek nerede bulalim? |
| Innkeeper, we want a meal | Lokandaji, yemek istiyoriz |
| Give me something to drink | Su istiyoriz. |
| Have you enough for all my men | Hepsi ichün kyáfii var mi? |
| Have you fresh eggs? | Tazé yumurteniz var mi? |
| Bring bread and cheese | Ekmek, ve penir getir. |
| Bring us coffee with sugar without sugar | Kahve shekerli / shekersiz } getir. |
| Hurry up, we haven't much time. | Chabúk, waktimiz kalmadi. |
| I am going to pay for it | Parasini verejeyim. |
| Bring us the bill | Hissáb getir. |
| How much do we owe? | Kach pára olajak? |

## Billets, Lodging and Stabling.

| | |
|---|---|
| I want quarters for men | Asker ichün yer ister. |
| Give me better quarters | Bundan iyisi yokmu? |
| Have you found me quarters yet? | Daha yer buldunuz-mu? |

| | |
|---|---|
| Where is the owner of the house? | Ev sahibi neredé dir? |
| Tell all these people not to be afraid. | Soilé korkmasunlar. |
| Light the fire, please | Lutfen, atesh yak! |
| Clear these houses; we are going to quarter our men in them. | Bu evleri boshaltmali; askerlerimizi oturtajaghiz. |
| I want stabling for horses | Atlar ichün ahúr isterem. |
| *Is the water cold here? (Is it feverish?) | Burada su so'uk mi dir? |
| *Is the wind good here? (Is it a healthy place?) | Burada hava iyi mi dir? |
| Have you small pox in this village? | Chichek illeti vár mi? |
| Tell me the house where there are sick men. | Söile bakalim, hanghi evda hasta vardir? |
| Thanks, we want nothing more now. | Teshekkür iderem bashka bir shei istemiyorim. |

\* Questions asked regarding climate.

### Strangers or Suspects.

| | |
|---|---|
| Stop or I shall shoot | Dur! yoksa atesh iderim. |
| Don't move from the spot | Bu yerden kimildama. |
| Stand a little further off | Dahá uzák dur! |
| Come closer | Yakin gel! |
| Turn round | Dün! |
| Put down your arms | Siláhinizi brák! |
| Surrender! take off your belt | Kemerinizi soi! teslim ol. |
| If you behave yourself you will be safe. | Rahat dursaniz, korku yok. |
| You may not talk to anyone... | Hich bir kimseye söile mé! |
| You are trying to deceive me | Beni aldatmak istiyorsiniz. |
| You are lying | Yalan söiliyorsiniz. |
| You are a spy | Jásús sin. |
| You are under arrest | Tahti-tefkifda-siniz! |

### Wounds or Sickness.

| | |
|---|---|
| What is the matter? | Né vár? |
| I am wounded | Yaram vár. |
| Where are you wounded? | Yara nerede dir? |
| Keep quiet | Rahat dur. |
| You mustn't speak | Konushmamalisiniz. |
| Sit down, lie down | Yát! |
| Undress yourself | Soyun. |

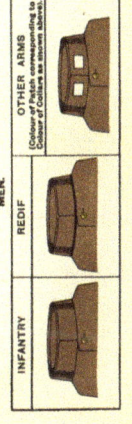

www.ingramcontent.com/pod-product-compliance
Ingram Content Group UK Ltd.
Pitfield, Milton Keynes, MK11 3LW, UK
UKHW021904240426
12048UKWH00045B/642